THE SYMBOL SERIES

OF

LECTURES

BY

MRS. CORA L. V. TAPPAN.

COMPRISING :

THE SYMBOL OF THE LETTER M.

THE SYMBOL OF THE CROSS.

THE SYMBOL OF THE TRINITY.

BOSTON:

COLBY & RICH,

No. 9 MONTGOMERY PLACE.

1877.

THE SYMBOL OF THE LETTER M.

A LECTURE DELIVERED IN CHICAGO, ILL., BY

MRS. CORA L. V. TAPPAN.

~~~~~~~~~~~~

Among a large class of modern realistic think-
ers, everything pertaining to mythology is resolved into a fable, and all tradition is pro-
nounced superstition. But the Positivism of
Comte indulges in a little transcendentalism by
accounting for singular coincidences on the score
that the tendency of all substance is to seek a
repetition of its former conformation, and the
tendency of all organized forms is to seek their
own likeness. Nothing can, in an intellectual
sense, be more nearly mythological than this;
and yet the Positivist school considers it the veriest philosophy.

If we escape from the narrow limits of mere
realism, we shall find that Nature herself is the
most symbolic of all possible existences; that the
very things which are most important in life are
only suggested externally, and that the forces at
work in the great vitalizing mechanism of the
universe are barely hinted at in what men see

(3)

and call reality. A sunset is suggestive of another day of glory on the morrow, and faint indications along the horizon are signs of what may be seen in the approaching tempest. The traveler perceives the indications, on the desert, of the approaching simoon, but he must first know the significance of the symbol that portends the approaching storm.

Every power and force in Nature reveals itself by a series of signs and tokens. Nature has no audible voice. She has not even an intelligible language interpreted alike to every understanding ; but he who would know may find her innermost secrets. To him who is blind, Nature is a blank ; earth contains no prophecy of future blossom and fruition ; the rocks are dead masses of matter, and the trees convenient for fire-wood and building of ships. To him who has no power of interpreting the signs of Nature, all splendors of sunset skies and starry firmaments are lost ; they have faded into insignificance—they are not.

The religion of the ancients was largely symbolic. Their language compelled this ; and the nearer you approach to the aboriginal or even the early patriarchal nations, the more do you find that their sublimest ideas were expressed in vague and, to you, unmeaning symbols. But it has been shown, not only by revelations in the various academies of science in Europe and by inscriptions which are now preserved in the European museums, but by every variety of source from whence ancient learning has been deciphered and unraveled to human understanding, that every character employed by the ancients,

symbolic, hieroglyphic, or otherwise, expressed
a thought, and that that thought is coëqual with
the intelligence of this century. Especially is
this true of religion. The religion of the ancients necessarily was symbolic. They lived
closer to Nature, and Nature expressed herself
in a different manner from what she does to the
scientific mind of to-day. You can get some idea
of this from the aborigines of your own country,
who believe in the Great Spirit, and hear his
voice in the thunder and in the wind ; who trace
their language in characters upon the bark of
the tree, or upon the skins of animals prepared
for that purpose, and who know by a single sign
or wave of the hand, what it would take a pro-
fessor in any college several paragraphs to ex-
plain in a scientific manner. The intuitions of
the savage bring him close to the truth at once,
and he can describe a battle by two men on horse-
back with drawn arrows and bows, better perhaps than all the poetry that describes, in Homer,
the battles of the Trojan gods.

Thus symbolism is reduced to the very crystal-
lization of human thought ; and an inscription
upon an ancient tablet, tomb or temple, may
mean all that it takes the sermons of this day, in
Christendom, to unfold. Ay, it may mean even
more than that: The sublimation of the very
thought of Deity.

You may be well aware that the sun, as a symbol of the divine mind, representing the thought
of Osiris, was the great Egyptian idea of worship. You may be well aware that Brahma is
typical in various symbols of Nature, and that
no form of life but in the East had its deific sig-

nificance. You will not forget that in interpreting these symbols the modern mind is too liable to interpret them with modern thought. But if you place yourselves in the position of the ancients, you comprehend that one image traced upon stone in the form of a serpent with wings, meant immortality, and that the ibis represented the undying nature of the soul, and that the sacred Apis, or Ox, represented the strength and power of the earth in its fruition each year, and that every form deified by them was but the symbol of the spiritual thought too subtle to be expressed in their language, but was veiled in this permanent symbol that the people might forever understand its presence and its power; that the departure, or idea of idolatry, crept in, but the symbols remain, as the solemn monuments of the age when out of wood and stone men carved that which would bring them to their knees in devotion, or uplift them to the stars in contemplation of the Infinite Being. People were not devoid of worship because they had idols. If so, we have little worship to-day. St. Peter's in Rome, and St. Paul's in London, are not exempt from the symbols of their worship, and if another generation should step in with a new form of religion and say, "Who were these Christian idolaters that had symbols of the cross, and inscriptions, and stained windows?" you would think it harsh, as a remembrance of the time when religion was supposed to be purely ideal and spiritual. And yet people drift into external expression without being aware that theirs may be the very idolatry that they condemn in others, because they imagine that while they worship, the spirit is there. May not others have worshiped with the spirit also, and in temples from whence the life has long departed, may not these once have been the fire and the fervor —Brahma with the three-fold image, Osiris with the eye of day, the various powers pictured by Osiris shining forth in flame and fire—may not these have been worshiped before the very shrine that you term idolatrous?

It is interesting from an æsthetic point of view, if from no other, to study the peculiar fitness of things in reference to these symbols, and to feel that everything, after all, shapes itself according to the law of poetic, if not of spiritual appropriateness, and that things have the right names mostly, and that the names express, in nearly all languages, the very idea intended to be conveyed. We think it was Hawthorne who said there are those who doubt the capabilities of language to express thought, mainly, because they have no thoughts to express; but, said he, the English language is capable of expressing the highest thoughts which the human mind is capable of appreciating or understanding. If this be true, then a symbol may express an eternity of life, and a battle-picture, in *basso relievo*, upon ancient marble, may convey the concentrated history of a nation.

Among these symbols that have been handed down with most singular significance, and that have had perhaps the most varied possibilities of interpretation, is the letter which forms the theme of our discourse to-night. Two triangles might be appropriately formed of a correct conformation of this letter. The triangle, in ancient days, when first discovered was used as an interpretation of the Infinite Mind who was supposed to be a circle, and therefore impenetrable except in this three-fold manner; and as we know that science gradually confirms this tradition, is it not kind to suppose that the ancients understood the true meaning of the triangle and circle, but used as a symbol the triangle and circle to picture the Divine Mind?

The letter M typifies also a symbol that was used in ancient Egypt to illustrate the rays of light, and the exact process of the sun's light crossing the equinoctial line was typified in this letter. It came to be at last a genuine character of the ancient language, and the interpretation shows that the most ancient secret order of which religious history furnishes any account, properly commences with the letter M, and that this order of Melchisedec denotes in the ancient interpretation the most secret and subtle of the powers of the sons of God. It is undoubtedly true that, although the first Hebraic record of this order begins with the time of Abraham, it was in Egypt first that the order originated, and was introduced to the children of Israel by the very power or person who is related to have met Abraham, and to whom Abraham so generously conveyed such a vast proportion of his treasures and possessions. This order undoubtedly was also the most ancient origin of what in modern times is known as Free-Masonry, a stated series of organizations that not only protected science, but also protected religion and life itself among the nations of the East; for you will remember that religion itself, as well as science, was veiled then in somewhat of mysticism, and that physical powers took the supremacy of the ideal. Hence it became necessary to clothe all expressions of science or religion in symbolism. The order of Melchisedec was undoubtedly a genuine order of recognized spiritual succession, and meant the transmission of spiritual power from one generation to another by a known theory or process of the soul's existence. Therefore, being subtle, all its mysteries could not of course be revealed to so simple and patriarchal a people as the ancient Hebrews. Yet, nevertheless, portions were communicated, and at last this order came to be regularly established among the Jews, and finally indicated a true succession of kinghood, priesthood and prophethood among them.

When, therefore, this true order was established among the Jews, it became certain that the Divine Mind intended to indicate the next Messianic period, and this period was one in the East that signified the millennium. You will notice that both terms Millennium and Messiah begin with the significant letter. The thousand years referred to in the ancient record undoubtedly did not refer to the real calendar, but to the Messianic period when it was supposed by the nations of the East that a new era would come. This period, from all computations that we can gather, must be about two thousand or twenty-five hundred years, between which periods of time the people of the East supposed that the earth by regular succession would be prepared for the next visitation of the Messiah. Thus Buddha in the East, thus the prophets among the Hebrews, thus the Messiah himself when he came and was acknowledged as such by certain persons, denoted not so much the personality thus anointed and nominated, as the fact that behind prehistoric revelations there was a symbol significant of such a period, and that that symbol must be what is now embodied in the letter M. The All-Seeing Eye, employed by Free-Masons as expressive of the Divine Mind, was none other than the Osiris of the Egyptians, whose eye was supposed to be the sun or light of day. This again was transferred to a spiritual being, the real Messiah of the East, who was supposed to come at various times and in various places, appearing as an all-pervading presence, having knowledge and power and judgment over the hearts and lives of men.

Surely, then, we have the key to many of those subtle mysteries that were supposed to be hidden and impenetrable, or to be merely idolatrous. This one character, traced through all the various languages, has perhaps more varied meanings, and is the beginning of more important words, than any other one letter or character in all the languages of the world. As the beginning of " Mysteries ; " as centering in the most sacred word which the English language knows of social relationship, " Mother ; " as typical of the millennial period when the Christ was expected to come, or the Messiah, in the East, and as denoting now the One Thousand which is the culmination of certain proportions of arithmetic figures—all these indicate a subtlety of poetic idea, and one which enables us to interpret with considerable degree of freedom and much spiritual leniency, the various symbols of the past. If

the divine Madonna of the Roman Catholic
church be transformed into the sublime Maia of
Jove or the veiled Isis of the Egyptians, the
Mother of the earth, and if we can understand
that spiritually the Madonna occupies the same
place that spiritually Maia did in mythology and
Isis in Egyptian religion, we shall then forget
our bitterness both toward the Roman Catholic
tendency to idolatry, and what we supposed to
be but heathen mythology. Minerva, the daugh-
ter of Jove, springing from his brow and fashioned as the Goddess of Wisdom, is also another
of the sacred words beginning with the same
letter, and typical of the fruition of that life
which gave to the Egyptians the subtlety of
meaning pictured in various forms and images,
but really meaning spiritual powers and forces
upon earth.

Why not Minerva as well as Mary ? Why not
the veiled form of the Egyptian Mother as well
as the Mother of Christ ? And why not all these
as well as the consciousness of the Infinite Parent, whose twofold existence overshadows the
Universe and makes life itself beautiful? Oh,
there is subtlety even in the employment of a
letter and a word, the varied meanings of which
shall charm the soul into consciousness of the
sublime possibilities of existence. Write all the
dear words that you know and the sacred symbols beginning with the letter M, and you will
have a sermon in itself that will reveal more of
antiquity, and ancient learning, and ancient
thought, than most sermons of greater profes-
sions. Write the name of the dearest object on
earth, and it will begin with the cradle where

the light of eye and the thought of love made that picture the image of divinity. No love so typical of the Infinite, none so recognized among ancient symbolism, as the love of the Mother, and none expressing to every heart so sweet a language and so uplifting a voice, bringing you nearer and nearer to the Divine Mind, by contemplation of her prayers and tears.

The Maia of Jove, beloved of him but not his wife, was the symbol of that subtle power that in the typical life of the spirit may link kindred souls together as brother and sister, friend and friend, in the great eternity. Mary, the name of the mother of Christ, is the symbolic name for love and sorrow, and expresses in its manifold ideas the very thought of what the Mother of the Son of Man should be.

Then if we find such revelations couched in ancient mystery, or glancing in a ray of sunlight, and if the lightning traces, as if by magic, some word or letter upon the heavens that means more than all things else, is not the spirit right in fashioning that interpretation to its dearest consciousness, and in making all forms of existence conform to the sacred and divine character thus revealed?

The true and typical meaning must be that of the millennial period, which period, as we have stated, according to the ancients, was once in two thousand or twenty-five hundred years; and one which the earth itself has come to consider as a portion of its regular possession. If it be true, according to the glacial theory, that once in about twenty-five hundred years the earth itself is subject to periods of inundation, and subject, also, not only to the precession of the equinoxes, but to variation of rotation ; and if Science can even problematically compute these variations to a certainty, and fix the period of time when the next deluge, for instance, will appear, then it must also become true that that which assumes for science the place of language (*i. e.*, mathematics,) must in the spiritual significance of symbols assume the position of spiritual truth, and we must look for much of our inspiration and prophecy not to the visible Christ, nor the actual cross, nor the sign of the crescent, nor the symbol of the sun, nor the Messianic emblems, but to the spirit of that which founded these symbols and made them mean the very soul of existence itself.

We know of no higher contemplation for the mind than to fashion for itself a single character or symbol, representative of that which is supposed to be most perfect ; and while idolatry is to be deplored, anything which can lead the mind to a loftier contemplation of the beautiful, even though it be symbolism, must be readily employed.   What characters are these (notes of music) that give such strains of melody when under the interpretation of a skillful master ? You would pronounce them cabalistic and strange, if unfamiliar ; but when interpreted to your understanding and senses by the magic touch of a master, behold what wonders in a simple scroll of written music ! Was it Mozart's Requiem that gave to the world such a sad refrain of a wonderful life ? And was it not in the very passion of the death approach, that he saw, as it were, with divine comprehension, and sang, as the swan

does, his own dying song? The world might
not know how a soul should go out into eternity,
if none could interpret the Requiem of Mozart.
So you may not know what sublime songs have
been sung to the ancient symbols that frown upon you from various obelisks and marbles and
tombs of the past. You may not know what
wonderful powers of thought and inspiration
were gathered in the pavilions where the ancients
worshiped and in Mithraic caves—again employ-
ing the significant letter—where the sacred tablets were preserved whereon were written the
very emblems of the heavens and the signs of
the zodiac. Ah! carefully must the student
tread, or, in the attempt to make all things real,
we shall burn the Requiem of Mozart, and never
hear the last song of Beethoven nor behold any
of the sweet monuments that have been left upon
the shores of time. We must take care, or modern
realism, to build a house, will ravish the past of
its sacred possession, and in visiting Jerusalem
or Rome, will tear down the very image of the
Mother of Christ to serve the purpose of blind
prejudice, passion, or paltry gain. We need not
worship the past. There is no necessity that
her forms be adored. The mother whom you
cherish, and who passes away into the dust, is
revered in memory, and the sacredness of the
past is that it is your mother. All that is good
and glorious of to-day has been hers. The germs
of the present were nurtured in her breast. She
gave the seeds of all splendid thoughts and prophecies to the world. She held in her loving
hands, in Egypt, in Persia, in China, in Jerusalem, in Greece, in Rome, the sacred seeds that have

blossomed out into prophecy and poesy and song. Christianity herself has grown out of these very monuments, and rose in splendor by the very symbols that she has sought to destroy. Puritanism here and in England, the Reformation with its fire and blood, have been all in vain to exterminate the sacred and subtle Memory which the Mother of all Mysteries holds forever for her cherished children.

You may desecrate the grave ; you may trample it under foot ; the flowers may be despoiled, but the great earth will revolve and the careful hand of the true interpreter of the mysteries of this great past shall make herself known ; her voice shall be audible in the present ; the children of the coming generations shall speak her name—the name of that blessed Mother of the past, who has given all things to the present, asking nothing in return but that her memory shall be cherished, and her sacred deeds and words be unforgotten.

Out of the tombs wherein the martyrs and saints have been buried, it is said that oftentimes some symbolic flower or tree upsprings. The red rose upon the breast of the crucified maiden, the white lily blooming above the grave of St. Agnes, and over there in Rome sweet flowers blossoming from the tombs of buried Christian poets who were not Christian to the interpretation of the authorities of St. Peter's and the Vatican. Behold how the eternal Mother of the Universe holds in her sacred keeping all these joyous memories that at last spring forth to the generation that has forgotten the hatred and the warfare of sectional and religious strife ! The poet makes religionists clasp hands, and the prophet gives a new interpretation to all symbols, and you bridge the great warfare of centuries by a token or a flower. Perhaps you have had a cherished friend in childhood who gave you some token of writing or flower that you carefully laid aside; and then in after years estrangement has sprung up, and differences, and you have drifted further and further from each other, as a child will wander away from the mother, she all the time remembering. Then upon a sudden, in some old drawer or book, you will find the sacred symbol hidden away, and straightway the tears will spring up, and the generous thought will prevail, bridging over the wide difference, until you are one with your friend again. So in religious conflict, when the passions of men blind them, as Catholic or Protestant, as Christian or Jew, to the great meanings of the sacred word, and when they forget the spirit in contesting for the form of worship, and when, blinded by prejudice, they torture the letter to unmeaning jargon, and in warfare and flame send each other through the fiery ordeal into the world of souls, behold, the kind mother covers the graves of all alike with verdure and flowers, and over ancient monasteries, and ruins of abbeys, weaves her fair vines as though the children of earth had never had battle. Then the student who has forgotten the warfare, and the seeker of truth who has never engaged in battle, visit these graveyards of the past, and behold how faithful and kind a friend is the earth itself. Not less kind is the spiritual memory that keeps alive all things sacred, holds them in the upper air until the conflict is ended, and showers them upon the world in new symbols of life and beauty. The violets you dig up to-day from their native soil, and scatter at random, spring up another year in various forms and places, and the things that you violently put from you, because of some blindness or prejudice, at last return in gentle benedictions.

The Motherhood of the Universe is as symbolic as the Fatherhood. The great power of spiritual life is, that the Divine Parent embodies both father and mother. And it was Theodore Parker who used to pray, "Our Father and our Mother God," as he does now with loftier symbol and diviner consciousness, seeing that the great universe is alive also with that loving thought, so like the mother, so typical of all sacred and veiled mysteries in ancient time.

These are the meanings written in cabalistic and uncouth characters upon many an ancient stone. These are the voices that speak out to him who visits ruins and ancient halls with an intent ear. He shall hear the memory of the spirit that hovers around in the upper air, pouring forth, in the voice of Isis, in the sweet veiled stillness of the Egyptian temples, the sacred and wonderful mysteries of life. He shall see where the maidens, clad in white raiment and with lilies in their hands, kept watch by the vestal altars, while the Mother of Truth spoke to the people. He shall visit Delphos and shall not sneer when they show him the altar and shrine wherefrom the oracle in veiled form spake to man. He shall know that from behind, some inspired maiden or priestess gave forth the voice of the spirit, and that the inspiration was like the Mother of Truth. He shall not laugh to scorn when, following Homer's tale, he reads of the wonders of Maia and Jove to whom worlds are born that blossom into spaces as shining souls; and Minerva, who under another name gives to the earth her wisdom and her justice. He shall not smile when he enters the halls of sacred worship in the East, and knows that the Mother Earth is typified in the blooming Lotus flower, upon which is traced the form of life and of immortality. He shall not deride when he enters St. Peter's and beholds the Madonna, the symbol of the Mother of Christ, imaged there. Really, the symbol is the most ancient and the most expressive of all symbols which the earth can yield out of the soul and out of the body of external religion, fashioning the image that pictures to the earth the form of the Mother of the Son of Man.

Behold we give you the sign! It is not of church, nor of state, nor of priestcraft, nor of kingcraft, nor of the rule of men, nor of the rule of earthly dynasties; but only of the magic power of that sublime love that can uplift the world and release it even from the thralldom of the engrossing senses.

How kind to your nation has been the great Mother of Freedom that presides, or is supposed to, over your destinies. She has wiped away the stains of your warfare, with sweet peace and blooming flowers, and upon the graves of Union soldiers and those of the South, this same Mother of forgetfulness and of memory weaves her garlands, while the souls are transplanted to immortality; and the nation glides gradually into this same forgetfulness, and only remembers that truth endures, that the Mother of Freedom is always kind even to those who slay her, and that she lives a thousand lives in the Memory and thoughts of men.

All sacred things become spiritual. No symbol can destroy them. They are transfigured, and stay forever in the sacred tablets of the soul, and though seasons come and go, and monuments perish, and from Egypt's dust there comes no sound, in the sublime stillness of the spiritual atmosphere a voice is made audible that tells of all she has done for the world, and from all the ancient storied places brings to the lap of the present her treasures and lays them at your feet. Though Rome and Greece, the Mothers of Art and of Philosophy, have faded, there comes from thence a voice that interprets to the mind of Plato, in the language of Socrates, the most subtle mysteries of the world, and the divine cosmos is pictured in the sublime image of whatever form of thought to them was most beautiful. From England comes the voice of the great mother-world, dead for many years, but speaking in new-found voices of Science, interpreting with another tongue and thrilling the church with a new-found life—not the church implanted by the harshness of the Reformation, but the new church that springs up spontaneously from the people, and infusing into that church, life and kindness and power, so that England, to-day, learns that her past history has been but a dark gulf—perhaps a sea of blood, which the beautiful in science, art and religion, must bridge over.

To-day, the living spirit has a double voice. It

is not fire and flame as in the days of Moses. It is not the stern Nemesis as in the ancient East. It is not even the fiery flame that came wiᴊh the voice of the love of Christ. But it is the new form of truth and love revealed to man, wherein the two-fold symbol, Man and Woman, shall forever bless and beautify the world. The Mother of the eternities speaks to the present age, and from the symbol of the snowy lily you gather the sacred meaning of her word, and you bear it upon your hearts and place it on each shrine, while all the world keeps silence in that temple where each human heart must forever worship.

THE SYMBOL OF THE CROSS.

A LECTURE DELIVERED IN CHICAGO, ILL., BY

MRS. CORA L. V. TAPPAN.

Far away in Egypt, along the mystic Nile, it was the custom in ancient times to rear indices designating the rise of the tide, whereby Egypt's kings might count the probable harvest of the coming year. As the sacred river was supposed to contain the elements of life or death, and as the deities were propitiated with reference to the harvest time, gradually this symbol came to be revered among the Egyptians, because just in proportion to the rise of the tide, so would be the fruitfulness of the harvest. This indication was in the shape of a cross, upon which was marked, from year to year, the gradual rising of the river or its decline. Subsequently this symbol was introduced among the sacred tablets and in the various places of worship ; not in the form of the Roman Cross, however, but of the letter X, which at last, also, was found to be a symbol of the angle of the sun's rays, the points representing two pyramids, one inverted, and the several other points the four corners of the earth.

Among the ancient Brahmins the exact cross, equal in its different angles, is worshiped as rep-resenting the four quarters of the earth, or the various directions from whence come the different divinities whom Brahma sends to govern the seasons. The north and the south, the east and the west, are the cardinal points, and therefore, when described, present the exact rectangular cross. These are objects of devotion not only at the various points, but at the various angles of coincidence, and represent the sciences in their subtle and occult meaning among the Brahmins.

If you visit the far Orient to-day, however, you will find this ancient symbol has been usurp-ed by another, and that in the various countries of India the symbol of the Crescent towers above that not only of the Brahminical Cross, but also of the Egyptian and the Roman Cross. The Crescent sign of the religion of Mahomet, usurp-ing the more ancient religions of the East, has reared its head, and there to-day indicates the fire and flame with which the Prophet of Mecca would have enforced his religion upon the nations of the East. Even in the sacred city of Je-rusalem you find symbols of all Pagan re-ligions, and the worship of the Crescent is greater there than that of the Cross to-day. Whether the Prophet who fled to Medina real-ly represents a religion or no, it is certain that his followers are numerous, that the influ-ence of his religion has been vast, and that with the fire and sword in one hand and the Koran in the other, the whole of the East has been devastated with rapine and murder at the hands of his followers. Whether you believe that the ancient symbol of the Cross was held sacred in Egypt or no, you will find that the indications are that the god Osiris, smiling upon the river-god, Nilus, below, represented the mystic symbol which was figured in the Cross, and that the veiled form of Isis contained the secret and subtle power whereby the ray of light enkindled the earth and made it fruitful. Whether you believe that in Mithraic cave and among the oracles at Delphos and elsewhere there were cabalistic and singular symbols, not only picturing the angle of the sun's contact with the surface of the earth, but also the different signs of the zodiac and their meaning, it still is true that upon those ancient tablets are found the symbols of science and many of those of religion to-day, and that the Cross itself is as old as are geometrical lines and figures in the science of the earth. Whether you believe that the cardinal points of the compass were indicated by the sacred symbol that we refer to or no, it is certain that upon every Brahminical temple is engraved the representation of the four corners of the earth and their various influences over humanity ; and that the followers of Confucius, in passing from the ancient faith of Brahma to the more modern one, and also the followers of Buddha, pictured these various symbols by lines, parallels and angles, among which the Cross is represented.

But it was left for the Romans to invent the Cross as a particular form of punishment, crucifixion not being among the ancient forms of punishment with the Jews, but various other means

of torture, as for instance, the Gehenna outside
the gates of Jerusalem into which were plunged
malefactors, and the fires of which were kept
burning forever; as for instance, their banish-
ment into the far desert, where it was supposed
the powers of death were abiding. The crucifix
was introduced as a system of punishment more
degrading because more public, and exposing the
malefactors to the gaze of the populace, who, of
course, they would wish to avoid and shun.

There was, as far as the student can determine,
no especial significance in the Roman Cross.
There does not seem to have been any intention
of a religious symbol of persecution in adopting
the Cross as the form of punishment, under the
Romish reign in Jerusalem ; nor does there seem
to have been in Rome, at least until after the
Christian Era, any especial significance applied
to the Cross; nor does it appear that in the first
two or three centuries of the Christian Era the
Cross itself was made the especial symbol of
what Christ represented, either of Calvary, of
his teachings, or of the especial meaning of his
mission to the world. It has come to be, however, typical of the entire Christian religion. It
has come to express in the great world of symbols an absolute idea ; and whoever sees or beholds the Cross upon temple or place of worship, or as an ornament in a niche or on the wall,
understands that it represents some special
idea of which " Christianity " is the symbol and
sacred term. Wherever this Cross appears, in St.
Peter's in Rome, on the walls of the maiden in
her cloister, within the charméd precincts of the
Protestant church in England, or upon the tem-

ples of modern worship here, it indicates an idea; and that idea must be either true or false ; must be either borrowed from the absolute revelation intended, or it must have become the symbol of an idolatry.

You call the Mahometans Pagan. They worship at the shrine of Mahomet ; their symbol is the Crescent. They have their orders of devotion ; they bow before the objects sacred unto them. This is Paganism. In the far East the Oriental worship prefigures the fire of Zoroaster or the sacred image of Brahma, and men bow before the graven images as objects of devotion, and you say they are Pagans. No voice has ever given to you the interpretation or the meaning of their symbols. No one has ever said to you that the Sacred Ox represented the principle of creative power, or that Osiris was pictured in the sun as the image of the divinity, or that the Brahmin does not really worship the images whom he names Brahma, Vishnu and Siva, but only the thought which they represent. Nevertheless, these are Pagan worshipers. Their symbols are not sacred, while over there in Rome the symbol of the Cross towers above St. Peter's dome, and that is called religion. Within this dome, that the art of the hand who fashioned it has made perhaps perfect as a work of architecture, are the symbols of the Mother Church of Christendom. Within this and other sacred temples are mirrored the images that Christians worship today. But Protestants declare that the Romish Church is idolatrous now, and that the symbols of saint and martyr and the glorious images of ancient art are paganistic compared to the sim-

plicity and severity of the Protestant faith. In
London, St. Paul's towers above the city, and
sends its bell-chimings through the ears of all
the inhabitants. The same symbol is there, and
within are nearly the same arrangements of worship, priestly robe and sacerdotal shrine. Yet
this is Christianity, and the other is Idolatry.
The Ritualists perform almost precisely the
same ceremonials with altar and shrine, temple
and robe, with the devotees at St. Peter's in
Rome. One is called idolatrous; the other, the
true church.

A few Quakers, anxious to escape from the
symbols that seemed to have no meaning, wrest-
ed themselves from the Mother Church of Rome
and from the Protestant Church, adopted the severity of sharps, angles and most subdued colors,
had no symbols and no sounds, no cross upon
temple, no adornment of walls or dwellings, and,
persecuted and ostracised at home, sought refuge
in a new world. To-day they consider the Protestant and Roman churches idolatrous, while
within their forms of silence and their walls of
colorless devotion they hope to receive the bless-
ing of the true Christ who is imaged in the Spirit;
shutting out the sunlight of day that the spirit of
truth may enter, and banishing the colors of the
flowers that the soul of heaven may descend
upon them. No music there, no altar and no
shrine, but a bare and barren cross rising upon
Calvary with piteous appeal to heaven and the
silence of the breaking heart that may not even
praise God in anthem and song.

A hundred years ago Dr. Priestley and others
introduced a system of more liberal worship,

wherein the Cross might represent a milder form of devotion than that of Luther and Calvin, and wherein somewhat of the love of God might shine through the bleeding wounds and crucified form of the Saviour. He was stoned in England; he was reviled in America. To day the Unitarian church rears its form side by side with the evangelical churches in Christendom, and has upon its towering height the symbol of the Cross. What does it mean? Idolatry in Rome, and not in the Unitarian church? Idolatry in St. Paul's, and not in the heart of the Quaker that preserves rigid lines and angles, and free even from a laurel bough? What does it mean that a symbol debased by one is exalted by another, and that the cross worshiped here upon this soil is more or less a symbol of Christianity than in Rome or in London it can be? Among the monasteries was one wherein it was claimed that a cross grew out of the moss-grown wall, shaping itself in lines of infinite beauty as the monks were wont to pray, and that upon this cross the very drops of dew that typified the blood of Christ were seen, and from them sprang the flowers that were his tears which the priests were wont to worship. The Rosicrucians held that they had discovered the one magic meaning of the dew upon the cross, whereby they might resolve all mysteries of life and death. Was theirs genuine and the monks in the cell idolatrous? Was theirs the truth because it was coupled with science, while in the monastery it must be considered as superstition? St. Catharine from Sienna crossed the mountains in midwinter that she might with her pleadings and prayers bring back the pope unto his people. Was this idolatry, and the poor cowardice of modern Christians, that will not cross the street in a rainy Sunday, worship? Is it religion that inspires men to deeds of cowardice, and is it idolatry that inspires them to deeds of bravery? Is it, then, true worship that stands in the midst of a Christian century wielding the weapons of avarice and pride and calling that religion; and was it an age of idolatry when saints and martyrs were driven heavenward through flame and torture?

What is it that inspires the souls of men? What is it that uplifts them from darkness and dross? What is it that melts and merges their lives into the sublime? Is it the name of the symbol they bear, or is it that which is traced upon their hearts as the impulse of self-sacrifice, and whether it be under the name of Brahma, Osiris, Mahomet, Zoroaster, Moses or Christ, anoints them as heroes, martyrs, saints, because they die for that which they believe to be true— better still, because they live for it and work out their lives in holy deeds and sacred symbols of devotion? Enough! Enough! We know what has been done under the name of the Cross. We have traced the fiery letters in seas of blood, and know there is no crime beneath the sun and no terror but what has been sanctioned by that symbol. You know that Protestant England worked as fearful ruin as Roman Catholic England. You know that France has been the scene of alternating horrors beneath the symbol that variously represented one sway or the other. You know that the Puritans fled from the symbol of the

Cross to rear the gallows on Salem Hill, whereon they might hang witches who did not believe as they did. You know that it is not two hundred years since it was unsafe for the freedom of speech and worship which you now enjoy to be even thought of. You know that it is not a hundred years since this meeting would have been impossible, and under the name of the Cross you would have been persecuted, if not with death at least with social and personal ostracism.

For the lofty deeds that are all unrecorded in history whereby some pale, wan faces, or secret and silent souls have wrought their way through fiery ordeals to glorious self-conquest, no flaming cross is there to blazon their triumph; no emblem is hung upon wall of cathedral or ancient abbey—no monumental marble rears itself above their graves; but indelibly upon the walls of life their tear-stained records have been wrought, and theirs is the crown that the martyr spirit must wear.

Let us interpret things according to their true meaning. If we have a symbol, let us have it mean something; and if it mean the Christ slain upon Calvary, let us see what its interpretation is to-day. Does it mean the shedding of blood and the slaying of innocent victims? Does it mean that in the name of the Prince of Peace countries shall be devastated and horrors perpetrated upon women and children? Does it mean that under the name of this symbol man shall wage war with his brother for the benefit of freedom, or his exchequer? Does it mean that because of differences of opinion there shall be slaughter and ruin, fire and sword, and that all the words spoken by the Master shall be forgotten?

Christ upon Calvary means the triumph of the soul over a brutal and selfish age; means the spirit conquering the flesh; means the triumph of God over the machinations of life below.

The bearing of the burden of the Cross is either a literal or a spiritual symbol. If a literal symbol, who follows it? Walk you the streets with burdens on your shoulders? Nay; you have beasts of burden, steam engines, electric wires, and fingers that die with toil to carry your burdens for you. A literal symbol? Who walks up to any Calvary to-day for any truth, even that which is most common? Evasion and falsehood, bickerings and strife, and a yielding to the everlasting pressure of that policy which hedges in the world, are the more usual methods. A literal symbol? Martyrs have died for the sake of its interpretation to their souls; but they would have been no martyrs if they had coveted the flame, the guillotine or the cross merely for the sake of martyrdom. He who aspires to be a martyr must not simply cut his throat, or hang himself upon the nearest tree, or stretch himself upon the physical cross. If he have nothing to die for he had better live. The soul understands that the meaning of the symbol on Calvary is, that whosoever would take up his cross and follow the Master must do so in spirit; that the cross of life to be borne is not necessarily of physical suffering, or of physical death or martyrdom, but is, if need be, that which plunged John Brown into the world of souls because of the love he bore for the slave, or that which gave to the nation a martyred president. These are the ways in which the Cross is the symbol of what the Master taught. If he but died on Calvary that the Cross itself might save the world through the shedding of his blood, then shall we forget that matchless message of the Sermon on the Mount, born of his teachings, and only follow this one image, the Cross. But if that was but the glorious consummation of a life whose purpose was to teach, to inspire and to uplift, the Elder Best Brother of humanity, who came to represent the possibility of man, then the Cross means the Golden Rule, the Sermon on the Mount, the teachings and the healings, the prophecies and the wonderful love that cast out all fear and blessed the little children and the Magdalen in one breath.

If the Cross means anything, it means that kind of victory and conquest over selfish pursuits and aims that brings the human life nearer to that standard which it typifies. If it means anything, it means the daily bearing of burdens that are necessary and needful to be borne, without complainings and without bitterness, gladly and willingly, because of the end of life to be attained. If it means anything, it means that the daily routine of existence that may become a care and terror and the veriest and severest burden, shall be gradually and constantly uplifted by the pervading presence of that sweetness of life, that perfection of existence which will make each burden seem light and every care sink into insignificance.

The truth is, that there is no cross to the soul that has gained self-conquest. Life itself has no

burdens ; care falls from you, and death becomes
the gateway of matchless life. What was the
cross to the Son of Man, whose inward eyes could
see into Paradise ? What was death to the saint
and martyr who above flame and the sacrificial
pile could see angels and hear them sing ? Nay,
nay ! That only is a cross which the spirit feels
is grievous to be borne, and which it is the intention of the divine economy you shall vanquish
in that very feeling. Go to your labor feeling it
a grievous burden ; see how it drags heavily upon
you, and weighs down your hands, and makes
you feel powerless. Go with the impulse of a
Divine love and a fervent desire to do good to
some fellow being, mother, sister, wife or friend,
and the labor is nothing, the toil becomes sweet,
and the hands are strengthened, and the feet become light. Ah, the vanquishing of life's burdens is the greatest cross after all.

If this symbol means anything to your understanding, it means it as applicable to your daily
life, to your individual existence, and the very
thing that is hardest for you to overcome, whatever that may be—pride, selfishness, vanity, external appetite—anything that stands between
you and the clearness of vision which the Master
had, is the cross that you have to bear and to
overcome. If it means anything, it means the
supreme control of selfishness and folly in the
world whereby the individual man is obscured,
and only his semblance appears in the daily life.

All cannot be heroes. Martyrdoms are not to
be bought at a price. You cannot walk to any
inquisition voluntarily. There are few opportu-
nities for heroic self-sacrifice. But the daily life

and the hourly vocation, and the things that lie all around the pathway—these multiply and become the huge cross and the burden that you have to bear, and which, if you bear triumphantly, leads you to the very crown of self-conquest and victory. To the true Christian this is the meaning of the Cross. All other meanings are idolatrous and Pagan. He who worships at that shrine or before that symbol without this meaning in his heart is an idolater. He who bows before it as bearing any veiled image of divinity, as God or man, and does not know the sweet message that it gives to the world, he is an idolater. He in St. Peter's who before the Cross makes the same symbol upon his person, yet does not know that it means self-sacrifice and self-conquest, is an idolater. And he who has piled up creeds large as the edifice in which he worships, bowing before articles and ordinances, forgetful of the one sweet message that makes life glorious, also is an idolater, whether he worship in Protestant church, at the shrine of St. Peter's, or away over in Pagan India.

We do not determine this matter for you. To ourselves there is but one interpretation. We must have no images that supersede the idea. We must have no temples that are greater than the souls that inhabit them. We must have no form of worship that supersedes the spirit of worship. We must have no Christ that is too far away for humanity to follow. We *must* have that divinity that enters the heart, shapes the life, unfolds the understanding, rears the edifice of existence—makes the glorious man or woman, all by its conquest and victory.

Matter is the cross; material life is the burden. All temptations that lie in your pathway, the various difficulties and obstacles of existence, the spirit must meet and triumph over. It is as glorious a victory as that which sent any saint or martyr into heaven; it is as triumphant when once attained. It brings the achievement; it is the resurrection; it is the life, the gradual, undying perfect sweetness and love that leads the human spirit through and over every pathway of difficulty unto even the triumph of death. Take your burdens from you? Not if we had the power this instant. Lessen your sorrows? Not if ours was the potent spell to drive them all away. A great and devout man said, "I have never had a sorrow that I could spare." Grievous to be borne? That is the very point. Hard and difficult to comprehend? That is the pathway to comprehension. Do not think that an infinite God of love could bring these difficulties. The tender mother never could make the stone pierce the foot of her boy; but he will never be a man unless it does. Do not talk of love that shuts in a closet the image where no breath can come. Speak not of affection that shields the tender plant until it pines away and dies. Speak not of that kind of love that gives nothing to strengthen the forest tree, but leaves it a sapling all its days. Wind and rain strengthen the oak, and even the violet meekly bows its head before the storm that gives the cooling draught to its eye of bloom. Tears in the eye strengthen the heart, and the hand is made glorious that traces its history over the walls of victory and conquest. A bed of roses is the fabled Oriental heaven and

paradise. The Christian has learned that the
sturdy pathway leading up the mountain height
is the one where the finest view can be obtained.
The tourist would scorn the tenderness that
would keep him always in the valley because he
might hurt his feet in climbing up where he
could see the sun rise over the Alps.

Climb if you would see the sun over the eternal
hills. Let the stones pierce your feet if you
would know what it is to have won the victory
of life. Do not push aside the thorns if you want
to know what it is to have vanquished them.
Mariners plow the seas; philosophers probe the
earth and dwell lifelong over one secret that they
may find out the mystery thereof. Hairs turn
gray, faces are wrinkled, forms become decrepit
over one truth that the soul is in search of.

The gold which will not last a single day when
you are dead takes your time, your attention,
your lives—you plod wearily to and fro every
hour of the day and count that not a cross. The
truth, however, God must reveal to you. Anything that is for the benefit of your souls must
fall down at your feet for you to pick up. Inspiration and prophecy and all spiritual knowledge must come without the asking! Go dig for
gold. Go plod your weary way along to build
up monuments that your children's children will
despise you for; but never say it is a cross again,
when just before you are golden truths and in-
spiring words that you would not turn your hand
over to attain, yet blame God for not forcing
them into your consciousness. Know that the
effort is there, the spirit is there, the light is
there. The way to it is across every temptation

that you shun, by the vanquishment of every foe
that you fear, the overcoming of the very chains
that enslave you and the bursting asunder of the
very ties that bind you. Know that the victory
is there, but it is not by avoiding any difficulty,
but only by surmounting it. The boy upon the
castle wall, the explorer in the North Sea, Dr.
Livingstone in Africa—these are what men will
do for an idea. Is not the truth that lies within the soul worth as much ? We say that you
will never have a spiritual treasure, a lofty truth,
a divine hope, a hallowed and consecrated fulfillment of prophecy, unless you win it across the
very chasm that you seek to avoid. We say that
the spirit cannot triumph over clay ; it cannot
win its destiny, cannot gain its inheritance, cannot understand itself, unless the glorious king-
dom of the spirit is outwrought of self-sacrifice
and pain.

Who prizes the titled nobility of Great Britain
or the Old World ? Who cares for the wealth or
fame that is handed down from father to son ?
Richard Cobden, John Bright, all the great
minds that stand up and plead the cause of men
are those who have won the victory of life for
themselves.

Who cares for fame written upon the ancient
tablets of any ancestral wall? You did not fight
the battles. Yours is not the credit for their deeds
of daring. What have you done? The test lies
here. The strength is in your own citadel. You
have made the castle which you inhabit. Your
spirit is there a sluggard and a dotard, or is alive,
alert, active, winning every day laurels that
kings and princes might envy. It is not needful

that the world shall see them. The soul is its own best and entire peacemaker. The soul can understand whether the *you* that inhabits the temple of your own life is a worthy occupant. The victories that you have won are traced there and your spirit understands them. They gleam out from your eyes and they light your face, and when a man meets you on the street, if you do not shun his gaze, if you look at him with a clear and honest eye, he knows that you have vanquished temptation and are not ashamed to look another soul in the face. Turn your gaze aside, look downward, and he knows that the victory is not won, and that the tempter is still there, that the serpent is still in the Garden of Eden, and that the man Christ has not taught his lesson to you, that God has not come to dwell in your heart.

Oh, take up the cross of life, bear it nobly and well, without shrinking, without terror, without fear ; not St. Peter's at Rome, nor Westminster Abbey, nor St. Paul's in England, nor all the churches that line the streets of your crowded cities, can give forth such chimes of joy and praise as go out from the towering height of that soul's sanctuary wherein the victory has been won over selfishness and pride and care, by the true meaning of the Cross.

Very Sincerely Your friend
Cora L. V. Richmond

THE SYMBOL OF THE TRINITY.

A LECTURE DELIVERED IN CHICAGO, ILL., BY

MRS. CORA L. V. TAPPAN.

The history of evangelical religion in Christendom seems to have been an effort to describe the Deity within certain limits of human comprehension; and the history of all religions may have been the same. The worshipers and teachers in Orthodox churches of Christendom have almost been at swords' points with the entire other portion of mankind with reference to the threefold expression of the Deity; and since, in a later day, the idea of the oneness of God has prevailed, incessant warfare of discussion, controversy and even bitterness has existed because of these differences of opinion.

Now, whether God be three or one, whether he be expressed in one form or another, whether man shall worship him through the symbol of the Golden Calf, or any image whatsoever that he may set up, cannot possibly matter to the Infinite mind, whoever and whatever that mind

(39)

may be. If man would only glide behind his prejudices, take off the mask of personal bitterness and strife, depart from his small individuality to the largeness of the universe, he would see that it is not the way in which he views the Deity that changes the Infinite, but that the method may uplift his comprehension, and that the Infinite may be three or one, a million or a single element, so potent and powerful that he is past the comprehension of man; but still, whatsoever furnishes a resemblance or a point from which man can view him, the Deity is willing man should employ.

Among the symbols that have expressed in the greatest variety of religions the Deity, there is none more used and more frequently found by the student of comparative religion than that of the triune attributes of Deity. It is a singular feature also in æsthetics that three represents not only an important number in harmony, but also the primal colors of the ray of white light—the threefold powers expressed in the rainbow, red, yellow and blue. All the varied harmonies of life are frequently expressed in a triune capacity. There have been periods in the earth's history when the biune Deity was the worshiped Deity of the world. The triune Deity, however, has had more followers.

In the Brahminical faith, you will remember, the threefold powers of Brahm are manifested or expressed in Brahma the Creator, Vishnu the Preserver, Siva the Destroyer of life. The three expressions of the Infinite form are worshiped, but the divinity expressed is not even worshiped or breathed among those of the Brah-

minical faith. A distinguished traveler, visiting
the Eastern countries, said to one of the noted
students of that portion of the faith adopted and
taught by Confucius, " Why do you not worship
Brahm and build temples to the Infinite? " He
replied, "Shall we insult the Infinite Omnipres-
ence with temples? So subtle is Brahm, the
spirit, that he abides in all essences and exists
everywhere. Does he not know our innermost
thoughts? But Brahma, Vishnu and Siva, are
the lesser divinities, the expression of the Deity
appointed to fulfill his work and perform his
task. To these we give our devotion, our praise,
our adoration, or our offering of fear."

This was an Oriental interpretation of a problem that has baffled the skill of all the theologians
in Christendom. This was arriving at a view of
the question entirely apart from that taken by
the Christians, who endeavored to comprehend
why the Brahmins did not worship and adore the
real Divinity instead of the threefold representation of it.

Hence, among the followers of this portion of
the Brahminical faith, there is no worship to the
Infinite Being whatever. They would not insult
the Infinite by offerings. They know that Omni-
potence requires none. But these expressions of
Divinity, the deities that they do worship that
are more within their comprehension and reach,
receive their various praises and oblations. It is
a singular fact that Siva, the Destroyer, has more
temples than Brahma the Creator, or Vishnu
the Preserver. It is a singular fact that fear
causes more devotion than love and confidence.
Men usually pray and fall upon their knees

when in terror; while in the midst of their joy and prosperity they forget the Divine hand.

Among the Egyptians the biune Deity was worshiped, represented in the form of Osiris and Isis, the two-fold forces and powers of the universe. But Osiris was not God; he was only the most potent and powerful representative of Deity —the God of the Sun's rays, veiled behind the light and splendor of the Sun, in whom was creative power. Isis was the earth, or the veiled mother of creation, holding in her secret heart all fructification and the powers of procreative life. The Egyptians, however, were the first to discover that the Deity might after all be a sphere of oneness; and it was among the Egyptians, we believe, that the first discovery was made of the only geometrical figure that would solve this infinite circle. Infinitude in the Orient was represented by a circle. The sphere with its winged serpents was infinitude and immortality. The circle represented the Infinite Mind. That mind or power had never been solved; and geometricians are aware of the one difficulty of measuring the sphere or of solving the problem of the circle. The triune Deity came to mean among the Egyptians the evolution of the perfect sphere of life, which was, of course, mysterious because a sphere. In the Mithraic caves and among the priests, who in Egypt were also the learned men and scholars, there was a necessity for veiling even science under the garb of religion, and so commingled were religion and science in those days, that the sphere which represented the Deity, also represented the perfect of measurement on earth, and the Trinity which represented the threefold powers of the Godhead, also represented the triangle, the only form of measurement which solves the circle.

Some persons, whose scholastic attainments are greater than their intuitions, believe that the entire origin of the thought of the Trinity was in the fact of these geometrical figures. Others believe that the two have traveled hand-in-hand together, and that the word "Jehovah," which was not the original word for Deity among the Hebrews, was borrowed from the sacred tablets of the Egyptians, the meaning of which, as you are aware, is the future, the present, and the past; which also represented the infinite circle of existence. This infinite circle, divided into these threefold powers and attributes, fashioned all there was and all there can be of the Infinite Mind. With such an interpretation it does not seem mysterious or strange that the threefold attributes of Divinity in solving the mysterious and perfect infinite circle could have come to be more worshiped than the circle itself. Since it is impossible, geometrically, for a complete sphere to be penetrated, there must be a point upon which the mind can fasten, and the first figure which probes the circle is the point, the only figure, as we have stated, being not the square but the triangle.

Therefore, geometrically as well as historically we can trace the secret meaning of these figures as understood by ancient priests and scholars who, desirous to veil their learning from the masses, adopted mysterious names and symbols of the Divinity, until at last the symbol came to represent the Deity, and the original spiritual meaning was forgotten.

Nothing is more natural, more in accordance with the wonderful spherical form of the earth itself, and the starry firmament, than that the sphere, the infinite circle, shall represent the Deity. Always among the Egyptians this was so. Always above their temples the winged sphere, globe or sun, occupied the most prominent position. Other and lesser divinities were represented in column and figure, but the sphere held supreme control.

The favorite form adopted for the building of the pyramids was the form of the triangle. Why? Because in the inundations of the river Nile any other form of building was liable to be overthrown by the action of the waters. The basic line being formed, and the two other lines being coëqual, there was no action of the waters that could destroy these structures. The building of the pyramids itself is a monument to the three-fold powers of the Infinite Mind when probed by outward science ; and the threefold structures representing the Egyptian idea in her period of greatest prowess and learning show what man can do under the inspiration and power of science toward penetrating the mysterious circle of infinite existence. It was undoubtedly intended by these ancients, among whom perhaps Cadmus and Memnon were the inspired originators of learning and science, and from whom descended not only the language but many of the external symbols and tabular representations—it was undoubtedly the original intention that these monuments should serve for the physical preservation of the people and their food, while at the same time they expressed an offering unto the

Divine Mind. The ancient city of Ion, or the City of the Sun, was in its turn an offering to the great spherical soul of existence, whose symbol was the sun's rays, and whose potent powers were felt all along the bed of the Nile in the fructification and beautification of the earth.

Therefore, we have but to trace these symbols to their ancient significance to know that they are neither profane nor idolatrous, but that the original import was that of comprehending what could not be understood save through the symbolic representation that we have referred to.

The word "Jehovah" introduced in the Mosaic record and in that mysterious compilation called the Book of Genesis, was not the original "God" or "Lord" worshiped by the Children of Israel, but was the "God" or "Lord" taught by the language of the secret order of Melchisedec which had its origin in the East, and which conveyed to the Children of Israel, or the ancient patriarchs of that nation and the founders of the order, the real meaning of the word "Jehovah," and the sacred symbol of its triune expression. Afterward it came to be adopted with a spiritual signification, and finally it was expressed or embodied in the Christian religion under the form which has been used since that time.

It is no fable to suppose that the Deity represents himself to man in a threefold capacity. We do not know any reason why he may not do so more than that the one beam of white light may not shine variedly in red, yellow and blue vibrations, and at the same time be resolvable into the original white beam of light. We know of no reason why the Deity may not be expressed in the threefold capacity as supposed by evangelical churches, and yet at the same time preserve the oneness of the sphere and the threefold powers expressed in the pyramid. It has been supposed to be a mathematical impossibility, and no end of ridicule has been showered upon the idea of Deity in his triune expression. If it were understood, the worship of the Deity in that manner would be just as admissible as the worship of Deity in any manner which the human mind can comprehend. We do not know of any reason why God may not be expressed in a threefold as well as in a *single limited* capacity. The human mind cannot grasp the Infinite. Christ is the representative of God and man even among the Unitarians. Why not then the threefold powers that represent Divinity in the expression of the Trinitarian idea? We do not say that it is necessary, or that you are enjoined to regard Deity in this way, nor that it becomes obligatory to do so, but we say that whosoever sees God in that light clearer than in any other, worships him as truly as he who sees him through a stained glass of his own fabrication in some other way. You have heard of the controversy between two friends who were gazing from different sides at a light. One of them declared that the light was red, while the other said that it was green. They paused in their discussion to settle the dispute by blows. After a while they discovered that they had been looking at the light through different colored glasses. And this is the real interpretation of all figures and symbols that man employs to represent the Deity.

Whatsoever is best adapted to your vision;

whatsoever your understanding shapes, is the manner in which God shines upon you, while you must know that behind the whole the supreme whiteness of the Infinite Soul is not immured by any angle, figure or form of expression, but only by the one supreme circle of whiteness of his own existence. This is the signification of all ancient symbols and records that stand now as everlasting monuments of the past pointing to a period of time when the Deity was understood and represented in different forms and manners, but still when that form of expression might have represented his soul as nearly as any form of expression to-day. God veiled in human form, the Father, the Son, and the Holy Spirit, representing the Divine Mind, are not impossible forms of worship for a devout believer ; and he who sees the whole of God couched in that divine humanity, still must be aware that that divine conception is brought down to his understanding, and that the Deity is the transcendent other Soul whom he has not seen and does not understand. He who breaks the rule of life for the sake of an individual symbol is an idolater. But he who sees in the manifold images of nature the Deity that is enshrined there, and worships not the sun nor the stars nor the fire nor the elements beneath, but through these worships the Soul that pulsates beyond, is no idolater. The Parsee worshiping before the sun's rays or the flame of fire, the Hindoo mother who plunges her babe into the mysterious stream that the soul of the child may be saved, the Mohammedan who, bowing in his temple at eventide, sees Allah in the departing rays of the sun, are moved upon by kindred sentiments : through all these manifestations of devotion the soul is borne upward to the Infinite in contemplation.

The soul that is enshrined in human form must have some representation of the Divine Mind within the grasp of that form ; and whether you confess it or no, every human being worships the Deity in the image of that form which is most sacred, most divine, most exalted; he is the mother's eye that bends above in love, he is the angel of your life in any human form, he is the ministering pastor who preaches the sermon, or he is the form of Christ upon Calvary, or the threefold image veiled in the expression of the Holy Spirit and the Sacred Dove. Every human soul has his or her expression of God ; and these expressions, according to the finite comprehension, cannot be the infinite circle, but only such portion of that infinite circle as is brought within the grasp of the finite mind. Whoever understands most of life, whoever worships most of the expression of Divinity, whoever sees God most in the most varied forms, doubtless is the truest worshiper. And whosoever can glide behind symbols and beyond forms, and see the essential spirit and feel the truth of that spirit within his soul, doubtless is the most devout and inspired believer.

The Christ upon Calvary calling upon the name of the Father, the saint in the cloistered cell, the symbol of devotion set high in all public places, the triune Deity worshiped by whatever name and form, have their uses and are the embodiments of human worship. And the veiled name of Jehovah, traced in Hebraic shrine and temple, handed down to Christian worshipers by symbols of expression that you know not of, also represents the true deific spirit.

But let us see how the ray of light is broken to human gaze. Let us understand that it is so, and that between man and Deity are no barriers, but only lines of interpretation and methods of thought whereby humanity comes nearer and nearer to the Deity. We do not recognize in these ancient forms and symbols, therefore, merely idolatrous expression; we do not see merely geometrical lines and their interpretation, but we see that these have been the stepping-stones whereby the finite mind had been brought nearer to the comprehension of the Infinite, just as the child's mind is led by degrees through the smaller problems to the loftier ones of life. This is the manner in which the Deity expresses himself to your understanding each day and hour; and the true circle of life itself is manifested in this threefold manner in the human being. No human soul is expressed in its completeness in the outward form and brain. You have the spirit, the mind, and the body; sometimes all three seemingly at war with each other. You have the expression of the physical form and its laws; you have the mind and its education and outward bias; you have the ineffable light of the spirit shining behind the whole and guiding as best it may the external expression of the existence.

You do not know one another. You never enter scarcely the charmed circle of that inward existence that lies behind these broken lines. You scarcely know of what your friend or neighbor is composed and fashioned in his inner life. You see the red, or the yellow, or the blue of his existence, and you exclaim, "Oh, what a red light!" or "What an imperfect nature is this!" Could you glide behind quietly and interpret with the language of the spirit, you would see that this is only one of his forms of expression, and that the real man is, after all, a complete circle, and that the life that is hidden is greater than that which you can see, and that it is often the colored glass through which you are gazing that prevents you from seeing the divinity that is veiled in him.

Did you ever suspect that the qualities and attributes that you give to others are but the reflection of your own condition of mind? That in a gloomy day or a cloudy morning the whole Universe is supposed to be out of joint, when it is only your own mind, and that after all in the kaleidoscope of human existence it may be the kind of eyes that you see with, or the frame of mind that you chance to possess, that gives to humanity such a cloudy and varied aspect? Did you ever know, in the circle of human life, if you but know the charm, and understand the spell and interpret it, that every human being has behind the cloudy appearance and behind the broken fragments of light, a clear beam of whiteness that might gleam out upon you? How frequently you exclaim of a friend, "I never could see what my friend finds in *that* person to admire." Perhaps you have not looked with the eyes of your friend. Perhaps the sympathy, the love or appreciation necessary to reach the qualities that were hidden have not been yours. You must remember that life is a great barrier, that the walls of sense rise up between you and the soul, perhaps, that you most love; and that to probe that wall and surmount those obstacles any key of interpretation which may be given you is valuable and full of aid. Let us illustrate: Here are two souls estranged. They may have nothing in sympathy; no word can be spoken between them. But in comes a laughing child, and straightway the joyous smile, and the sunny eyes, and the dimpled cheeks, and golden curls make up a point of sympathy, and those who were strangers before, laugh and smile with the child. Shall we not be content to have the Deity interpreted to us through a little child? Shall we not be content that the symbol of the dove represent the Divine Spirit and the holiness brooding above? Shall we not be content that any lofty thought or any bond of human sympathy bridge over the space between soul and soul, and therefore bridge over the space between man and Deity?

Let us not mistake these useful symbols. Language is necessary for human expression. Souls do not yet speak face to face. And are not these given as the language of the spirit? Are not all sacred symbols given as the alphabet of the soul whereby we may come one degree nearer to the Divinity? Shall we cast aside the alphabet? Shall we not rather weave it into most beautiful forms of expression, making a complete language, so that all nations shall be linked together by this one tongue, so that we may know that Parsee and Hindoo, that the Brahmin and the Buddhist, the Mohammedan and the Jew and the Christian, have, after all, a common language of expression and thought, and that we have simply mistaken the symbol for the spirit? Shall we not avail ourselves of all the offerings that are given in Nature and Art to make a shrine and create a representation of Deity, expressing just as perfectly as to human life is possible the perfection which was intended by outward life? Shall we rob our gardens of their flowers? Shall we cut down the roses and the lilies because they are but symbols after all? Shall we not rather weave them into garlands of beauty and let them speak with their manifold tongues of praise, and on the incense which rises from their sweet chalices let our own prayers and offerings float?

St. Peter's in Rome, the temple that rears its head to heaven in your own land—whatever shrine or sacred place is builded, if that be the only avenue of reaching Deity, let us make it beautiful. We will not tear away from the walls one image. We will not take from altar or shrine one emblem of worship. No saint shall be removed from the niche or cloister where they have been lifted by human praise. We will not take one of the stepping-stones away from mankind whereby they reach Deity. So you do not stumble over the stone; so you do not stop upon the threshold; so that the outward vestibule be not mistaken for the altar; so that the shrine be only the means and not the end, let us have the incense, let us have the Te Deum and the glorious praises and songs in temple and church, let us have the choral service and all church ceremony, but let us not mistake the language for the thought, the alphabet for the full expression of the spirit. Let us only use these as the means of singing and praising, and expressing Deity in the loftiest form. If you were pupils and we were your teachers, and we wished to have you understand that a circle could be divided, we should of necessity, according to the rules of instructions, be obliged to introduce you to the triangle. Any teacher, parent or instructor, is obliged to make the child understand that the blocks of wood which are only symbols represent the real things for the time being, and that these are to be divided, added and multiplied until the child understands the meaning of addition in the brain itself. Now, every form of expression which Deity has ever been veiled in, Buddha, Moses, Jesus—all are but the blocks of wood, the stepping-stones, the sacred symbols, the ray of light that is to guide and lead mankind to a consciousness of the Infinite. We will have these preserved. We will wrest from the idolatrous forms that have been introduced, these sacred symbols. We will not allow them to sink into obscurity, leaving only the bare and barren walls of existence that have no meaning and no record.

No man has any right to desecrate the image of the cross to idolatrous uses. No one has any right to make the Trinity answer the purposes of the Infinite Spirit. No one has any right to say that a temple shall be devoid of beauty because St. Peter's has been desecrated, or because the churches of the East have become the means of idolatry. Christ scourging the money-changers in the temple at Jerusalem, is a figure of that form of expression that should drive from sacred images and symbols everything idolatrous and everything unworshipful, and make them mean the very things that they meant in the foundation of the language.

Let us have our symbolism. Let the temples of human praise and human love be adorned with loveliness. Let column, and spire, and dome be reared to the uses of existence. Let us have no charnel houses and tombs for the expression of love and praise; but the joy, and the melody, and the grand archives of the past—let these be restored in their original significance and meaning. We will have the rainbow, whatsoever the Pope may say, or whatsoever science shall rob that symbol of. The threefold light of the sun's rays means, if symbolized, Hope, Aspiration and Immortality. No matter if science declares it is but the prismatic reflection. No matter if the drop of water is resolved into three principal gases, we still have in the drop of water the symbol of the universe, and in the rainbow the triune expression of Deity, and in all sacred forms and images that which is beautiful and lovely. Take from the human mind all expression that ideally conveys that mind toward the beautiful, and you rob life of its supremest language; you take away the only good and perfect gift which fashions the language between you and God. Martyrs in dungeon cells, Puritans suffering the tortures of exile and death, the Quakers driven from their form of worship, are the severe expressions of what an unbeautiful religion can bring to mankind.

Ay, we may have our quietude, our cloistered

cells, our bare and barren walls ; but let these be when the soul is devoid of beauty, and has no loveliness of expression to give to God. Sackcloth and ashes for repentance, but for the world of praise let us have flowers, and sunlight, and song, and happy voices of children, and men and women singing their praises to God as though they were not ashamed to live. For crime let us have the tortures of conscience, the inquisition of the spirit judging its own action. Let us have the secret corner and the cloister where the soul may be tortured into discipline by its own consciousness. But for the love and praise of the Infinite, let us have the broad circle of the sun's rays, the clear, bending sky, the interpretation of all beautiful signs and tokens ; let us have pictures, statues, living images that shall express the poesy and harmony of being, and the threefold hues of the rainbow of existence blended and interwoven into every form of life.

A greater pyramid there is to build than any which Egypt holds. Her sacred and solemn river flows far away over desolated plains, and the silent fingers of those wonderful structures point evermore to the heavens which man could not fathom nor understand. Science has since probed the sphere, and the manifold arts of life have given to existence the charm even of almost the infinite circle.

The threefold form of Art—painting, sculpture and literature—has given to the world of external learning what the threefold form of spiritual worship gave in the Past. It was Del Sarte, in France, who gave to the understanding in art what was given in the interpretation of the religion of Christ by the early teachers of the Christian religion. It now remains for a magic hand and master mind to interpret to the understanding of humanity the every-day of existence, so that it shall become as beautiful, as perfect, as harmonious, as the threefold light that blended together makes the perfect whiteness.

We will sing you a song. It shall be fashioned of all sacred words and images that the world has ever known, and Jehovah shall no longer be dumb and distant and far away, but within the heart of every human being, veiled in the threefold attributes of love and truth and wisdom there. We will sing you the song that shall show that the threefold light of the Divinity is not enshrined in some distant sphere, but is in every human heart, waiting only for recognition there and expressing itself in whatever form of loveliness the human mind can understand.

Take this triune expression, love, truth and wisdom, and you will find there a solution of all the problems and qualities of life. We will prove it to you. You say this man is charitable, another is beneficent, another is kind and gracious ; but Christ's love is the fulfilling of the law. Whosoever loves his fellow being is kind, and gracious, and charitable, and considerate, and beneficent. Is not love the basis of the pyramid ? Wisdom : You say that such a man is just, and such an one has correct ideas, and that this one has knowledge ; but is not wisdom the embodiment of the whole ? Does it not include knowledge and learning, art and all that there is in human government ? Is it not that supreme wise beneficence that shapes all law to the single fulfillment of a wise and perfect purpose? Truth: Clear as light and crystal as the starry heavens. You say this one has integrity, another has honor, another has probity. Is not truth unqualified the representation of the whole? If you have truth does it not shine out in every deed and word, undimmed and unqualified? We give to your understanding the interpretation. These are the primal attributes of the human spirit. They are variously broken to your outward gaze, clouded it may be; but glide behind and you will find that the basis of all spiritual life is represented in these threefold words. Then if you will have the complete circle, if you will understand what the Divinity means, you must know that it means nothing that can be shaped in attributes, but is the perfect state of being. Christ said, "Consider the lilies of the field, how they grow. They toil not, neither do they spin. But I say unto you that even Solomon in all his glory was not arrayed like one of these." We say that a single perfect life unconscious of any effort or attribute expresses the Deity, while he who strives to be good, that he may gain happiness, falls short a thousand-fold of the mark. The lily in its whiteness, the rose in its perfect bloom, the heart of man shining out among his fellow-men with unqualified light and glory, not saying, "Is this truth, or is that falsehood?" but knowing no other way possible than to speak the truth, live the life, do the thing that is beautiful and glorious—this is the expression of the attributes of Divinity. This is the Christ, under whatever name or form you may worship him. This is the God made manifest to the human understanding.

Oh light of suns and stars, veiled by space and by time, the drop of dew in the chalice of the rose reflects the starry firmament, and man in the spirit of his truth, and love, and wisdom, reflects the Infinite. Let us no longer wander in the dark. Let us not clutch at phantoms, but see where God smiles face to face in every human being. In the eye of the babe, in the eye of the mother's love, and in the honest countenance of your fellow-being you may find enshrined the image that you have sought in vain through templed dome and ancient hall. Oh, let us build a temple. Let its foundation stones be of love. Let its two-fold sides be fashioned of truth and wisdom. Let the various portions be made of human existence. Let the device be crowned and glorified with the immortal consciousness of life, and let us not have brazen images, nor golden calves, nor any form, save that which shall interpret to us the understanding of the Infinite as expressed in man. Let us make humanity the shrine. Let the forms of worship be love and kindness, inspiration, beauty and everything that is lovely and beautiful in nature. Let us rear in foundation and in edifice such form of devotion as shall reach the very heavens in its spiritual height, and become merged in the Infinite by the very type that it expresses of infinite existence.

THE SOLUTION

OF ALL THE

Perplexing Problems of Life is to be found in the

SERIES OF LESSONS GIVEN BY THE GUIDES OF

MRS. CORA L. V. RICHMOND,

ENTITLED

THE SOUL;

ITS EMBODIMENT IN HUMAN FORM.

IN SIX LESSONS, VIZ.:

1st Lesson.   The Soul; its Relation to God.
2d Lesson.   The Dual Nature of the Soul.
3d Lesson.   The Embodiment of the Soul in Human Form.
4th Lesson.   The Embodiment of the Soul in Human Form—(Cont'd.)
5th Lesson.   Tne Re-united Soul, including Parental and Kindred Souls.
6th Lesson.   Angels, Archangels, and Messiahs.

The primary object in the preservation of these lessons in book form was to answer the urgent request of members of classes for a text book or book of reference; but the ever increasing interest in these and kindred subjects among thoughtful minds in all parts of the world, and the great demand for information concerning the subject matter of these teachings, have led to the publication of this volume.

Handsomely bound in Cloth.   *Price, $1.00.*

All orders addressed to **WM. RICHMOND,**
ROGERS PARK, ILL.

*Nobody practicing or making a study of the occult laws
governing healing should be without a copy of the*

NEW BOOK,

PSYCHOPATHY;

OR

SPIRIT HEALING.

A series of Lessons on the Relations of Spirit to its own organism
and the inter relations of Human Beings with reference
to Health, Disease and Healing, accompanied by
Plates Illustrating the lessons.

BY THE

Spirit of DR. BENJAMIN RUSH, through the Mediumship

OF

MRS. CORA L. V. RICHMOND.

SUBJECTS OF LESSONS:

Lesson I.   The Physical and Spiritual Basis of Life.
Lesson II.   The Influence of Spirit over the Organic Functions of
the Body.
Lesson III.   The Influence of Food, Raiment and Surrounding Con
ditions and Atmospheres upon the Human Organism.
Lesson IV.   Psychology, Mesmerism, Magnetism and Electricity as
Healing Agencies.
Lesson V.   Social Life, including Marriage and Parentage.
Lesson VI.   The Actual Magnetic Poles and their Corresponding Nerve
Centers; their relation to Psychopathic Treatment.
Lesson VII.   Volition.
Lesson VIII.   Psychopathy.
Resume.

Handsomely bound in Cloth.   *Price, $1.50.*

Address all orders to   **WM. RICHMOND,**

ROGERS PARK, ILL.

Is Materialization True

WITH

ELEVEN OTHER LECTURES

OF GREAT INTEREST.

GIVEN IN CHICAGO, ILL., BY AND THROUGH THE
TRANCE-MEDIUMSHIP OF

MRS. CORA L. V. RICHMOND.

Spiritual Spheres

FOUR LECTURES

DELIVERED (IN TRANCE) BY

MRS. CORA L. V. RICHMOND.

COMPRISING

THE SPHERE OF SELF:

THE SPHERE OF BENEFICENCE:

THE SPHERE OF LOVE AND WISDOM:

REVIEW OF "SPIRITUAL SPHERES."

BOSTON:

COLBY & RICH, PUBLISHERS,

CORNER OF BOSWORTH AND PROVINCE STS.

1886.

LIGHT OF TRUTH
1897

Prominent Workers
of Spiritualism

Cora L. V. Richmond

The subject of this sketch is, perhaps, next to Andrew Jackson Davis, the most universally known worker in the Spiritualistic ranks. Mrs. Richmond has been in the field about forty-five years, having begun her career as a speaker when but just entering her teens, though born a medium. She is still a fine looking and vigorous woman, and much admired by a large following. Her influence as a speaker is to awaken the higher emotions in her hearers, and leave an impression never to be forgotten. Her inspirations are highly philosophical — often beautifully sublime and elevating in the extreme. Her poetical improvisations, both as prelude and peroration, are calculated to touch a tender spot in the hearts of the most callous or indifferent. As an individual she impresses with earnestness and elicits sympathy, due, perhaps, to her mission as a medium and revelator — a mission not leading up a path of roses — and intuitively felt by the more sensitive of her hearers. As a worker she has filled every department in our cause — society leader, organizer, pastor, missionary, comforter, teacher, guide, and representative — as most of our constituents know by newspaper reading during the past. A London paper says of her : " Mrs. Richmond is an inspirational medium whose life has been spirit-guided since girlhood. She did valuable work in London and the provinces upwards of twenty years ago. Her long record of public labors for spiritual truth is a noble tribute to her high character and the wisdom of her spiritual guides, philosophers, and friends."